Beauty Tips

10 Minute Makeover

A collection of fabulous beauty tips to release the goddess within!

(im)PulsePaperbacks

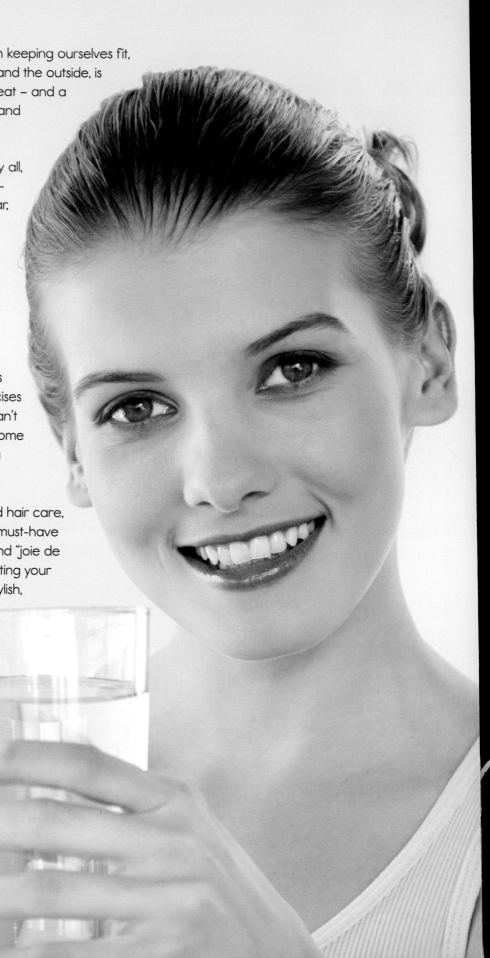

Investing well-spent time and energy in keeping ourselves fit, healthy and happy on both the inside and the outside, is our finest ally in looking and feeling great – and a well deserved expression of self-care and positive self-image.

Inner and outer beauty is attainable by all, regardless of age, size, shape or style – and it doesn't have to come out of a jar, over a counter or in outlandishly expensive treatments.

This book is an easy to use guide in achieving inner calm, improved health, enhanced physical energy and sparkling radiance!

Combining tips on relaxation and stress relief, energy boosting ideas and exercises with healthy eating 'superfoods', you can't fail to give your mind and body a welcome replenishment of nutrition, vitality and a tranquil sense of wellbeing.

Fabulous tips and remedies for skin and hair care, timeless fashion "Do's and Don'ts" and must-have beauty tips will polish off your new found "joie de vivre" and benefit you further by boosting your confidence and releasing that uber-stylish, self-assured and relaxed Goddess within!

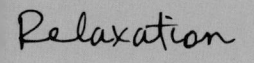

Relaxation

One of the easiest ways to make a change to your well-being is to plan "you-time" in which to relax and unwind. Relaxing calms anxiety and helps your mind and body recover from the everyday hustle and bustle, which can cause stress. Music, a long soak in the bath, or a walk in the park are great ways to relax.

Regularly using a relaxation technique is an easy and effective way to relieve stress and achieve a deeper sense of calm and wellbeing, for both mind and body.

The practice of relaxation techniques can improve how you physically and emotionally respond to stress by lowering blood pressure, slowing the heart rate down, reducing muscle tension and other associated ailments such as headaches and feelings of anger and frustration. Regular relaxation increases energy levels, diminishing the unpleasant symptoms of anxiety.

Relaxation technique

Firstly, minimise distractions, such as turning off the TV or radio and unplugging the phone. Give yourself permission to ignore the doorbell and to deal with the next job or chore later. This is valuable 'YOU-time'.

Sit or lie down in a comfortable position, preferably in a quiet place where you won't be disturbed. Close your eyes and begin to breathe slowly and calmly, inhale through your nose and exhale through your mouth. Notice the rhythm and speed of your breath and slow it down if necessary.

Beginning with your feet, tense and simultaneously relax each part of your body, putting enough tension into your muscles to make them tense but not so that they are painful. Working your way up through your legs and torso tense each muscle eventually ending with your face and head.

Whilst tensing and relaxing each part of your body be aware of your breathing and focus upon the warmth and heaviness of your muscles as you let go of all your tension. Affirming thoughts may help to achieve a deeper feeling of relaxation; "I feel calm and quiet. My body is heavy, comfortable and relaxed. I feel at peace".

Empty your mind, pushing any current distractions or worries to the back of your mind - simply let them float away. Sometimes the visualisation of a calm, relaxing place can be helpful such as a scenic view of a sprawling summer meadow or a sandy beach with the waves lapping at the shore.

Stay in this position for about 20 minutes, then take some deep breaths, open your eyes but remain sitting or lying for a few more moments before getting up.

For relaxation techniques to be of optimum use, it is a good idea to make space for them in your everyday life.

Coping with stress

Having a little bit of stress in our lives isn't a negative thing; small amounts of stress serves to mobilise our bodies providing us with the necessary energy and verve to take us through the process of coping with challenges. However, having too much stress in our lives can lead to a wide range of health problems including, upset stomach, headaches, depression, anxiety attacks, high blood pressure and even conditions as serious as heart disease or strokes. Stress is a normal part of life and as such we can worsen the symptoms of stress by giving ourselves a hard time for even feeling them in the first place.

So first and foremost, be easy on yourself - self-criticism will only expend unnecessary energy and make an already stressful time harder to deal with.

Stress relieving tips

Be kind to yourself, do something relaxing that you enjoy on a regular basis, such as taking a scenic walk or treating yourself to a candlelit bath whilst listening to your favourite CD.

Alcohol
Don't reach for alcohol in times of stress, it may bring short-term relief but alcohol is a depressant and will inhibit restful sleep, as well as the added strain of having to deal with processing toxins through your system the following day.

Aromatherapy
An ancient Chinese tradition, aromatherapy is based on the healing properties of plant extracts which are bottled as 'essential oils'. The oils are inhaled and circulated through the bloodstream, having an effect on the release of the hormones and emotions of the user. For example, Lavender oil is used to help in relieving stress, tension, mental exhaustion, anxiety and agitation.

Breathing
Be aware of your body and breathing, notice any tension in your muscles and breathe deeply, gently stretching out and relaxing your muscles.

De-clutter
Mess adds to confusion and feelings of powerlessness so de-clutter!. If you are surrounded by clutter and disorganisation be dynamic and have a good clear out and tidy. You will get a sense of satisfaction and feel far more in control.

Diary

Keep a journal – or a stress diary. Some people find that writing down their thoughts and feelings can be extremely helpful, and an effective way of putting their problems in perspective, or in coming up with solutions to solve the problems they are experiencing.

Diet

Eat a balanced diet for a healthy body and mind. When our bodies are nutritionally boosted we possess a greater capacity for dealing with the effects of stress.

Easy on the eye!

Place something you really enjoy looking at in optimum view in your house or room, perhaps fresh flowers, a favourite picture or a treasured ornament.

Exercise

Exercise regularly; physical exercise has great benefits in managing and reducing stress. Exercise is a fabulous stress buster and you don't have to be a gym dweller or high-impact cardiovascular devotee to reap the benefits from regular exercise.

Just 20-30 minutes brisk walking 3 times a week will reduce stress and help aid more restful sleep. This can be either be maintained or increased over time depending on your fitness level and ability.

Exercise relieves stress by allowing the body to release pent-up tension and frustration - relaxing muscles and raising the level of endorphins within the brain, which are our 'feel good' chemicals.

Taking regular exercise mobilises our bodies, keeps us in a better state of health and consequently makes us feel good about ourselves. Take up stress relieving relaxing exercise such as Tai Chi or Yoga, which are renowned for their relaxation qualities and techniques.

Meditation is another popular method of relaxation and effective stress relief. It has become a part of our popular culture and due to its positive; and often immediate results, is often recommended by Doctors for reducing stress and pain management.

Meditation involves sitting in a relaxed position, closing your eyes and clearing the mind, focusing upon your breathing, an image, word or sound, which allows you to be distraction-free and completely relaxed. The practice of meditation lowers the heart rate, slows down breathing; thus using oxygen more effectively, and lowers blood pressure. This process of mind clearing and relaxation is thought to promote feelings of being deeply rested.

Why exercise?

If you can't function in the morning without gallons of coffee and you run out of energy by mid afternoon, then you need to look at simple ways of boosting your energy levels through food and exercise.

Our bodies are designed to move. When we're not in motion our circulation and energy systems slow down, making us feel lethargic and even less likely to want to mobilise ourselves.

Exercise is a fantastic way of boosting our energy levels and revitalising the whole of our physical and mental wellbeing. We feel less tired, less stressed, happier and healthier. From the very young through to the older generation, exercise is an important activity in our lives and age & fitness appropriate exercise routines can provide much needed 'get-up-and-go' and an enhanced quality of life.

You don't have to jog, run or take part in high impact aerobics should they not suit your sensibilities or physical abilities - although they do have certain health benefits they can also be harsh on joints and muscles and cause wear-and-tear in the long-term. Low impact exercises can be just as beneficial; and very enjoyable too! Many of us hear the word 'exercise' and groan. Exercise is often associated with painful, energy-sapping activities which drain our bank-accounts through well intentioned, but ultimately severely underutilised gym memberships. Consequently, we often end up blocking our willingness to go anywhere near anything remotely looking, or sounding, like an activity which might need some form of physical exertion.

So choosing exercise that we can enjoy is important, as is how we program ourselves to think about exercise. If we think negatively, we will see exercise negatively. So try some more positive thoughts such as "It feels really good to exercise", "I love going out for a long walk in the morning" or "I really enjoy my dancing class".The more you can think positively and program yourself to enjoy exercise, the easier it will be to overcome those negative thought patterns.

Aqua aerobics

This is the performance of aerobic exercise in shallow water such as a swimming pool. One of the many benefits of performing aerobics in the water is that the water provides support for the body which reduces the risk of muscle or joint injury and because the exercises are usually performed in chest or waist-deep water, you do not have to be a swimmer to participate. Water-related exercise increases cardio-vascular fitness, as well as improving overall strength. Aqua aerobic workouts usually combine a variety of different techniques, mainly taken from land aerobics. The workout also may incorporate special water devices that can be used in the water to aid in resistance or flotation.

As water provides more resistance than air, in general aqua aerobics will expend more energy than many land-based activities. An aerobic water exercise of around 30 minutes will help burn about 300 calories.

Cycling

Cycling is an enjoyable form of low-impact aerobic exercise with many health benefits, including weight loss, improved overall strength and muscle tone, enhanced stamina and coordination, lowered risk of heart attack and stress reduction. For safety and security, always wear a helmet and reflective or light clothing if cycling at night or in the dark.

Dancing

Experts say that dancing burns calories, boosts energy, improves circulation and tones muscle leading to increased strength, endurance and flexibility. In fact, dancing can burn just as many calories as other, more "traditional" exercises and in addition, dancing relieves tension and stress, improves your mood and serves as an outlet for your creativity. Dancing also is convenient and you don't need any expensive equipment.

Running

Running - you either love it or you hate it; but the health and well-being benefits of running should outweigh the hatred! One of the most common reasons that peope run is to lose weight or get fit, and then to maintain a healthy lifestyle. Running also prevents muscle and bone loss that occurs naturally with old age and may also help fight disease; it certainly helps to strengthen your heart and whole cardio-vascular system. There are also numerous proven psychological benefits to running as it can help build confidence in all ages of people. Going for a jog can reduce your stress level drastically - and of course, endorphins are the body's natural antidepressant. It is though easy to strain muscles and suffer other injuries whilst running, so it is important that before undertaking any training programme you discuss this with a doctor or fitness professional and ask their advice about a regime best suited to your abilities.

Swimming

Swimming is one of the all-round most beneficial exercises we can undertake, working all the major muscles and massaging the internal organs in the process. As the density of the human body is similar to that of the water, the body is supported within the water and therefore less stress is placed upon joints and bones. Swimming on a regular basis builds stamina, muscle strength and tone and improves cardio-vascular fitness.

Walking

One of the most accessible forms of exercise is walking. The beauty of which lies in its ease and flexibility. Walking can be done alone, in a group, indoors, outdoors - it can be fitted in between break-times at work, leisure time in the evenings or weekends, or even as a regular morning ritual. Improving the oxygen capacity of the lungs and heart, walking briskly for 20-30 minutes 3-4 times a week has an invigorating effect on energy levels and circulation. To continue improving the benefits of walking, increase the pace and duration over time.

Skincare

Our skin is the world's window into our personal health, vitality and emotional wellbeing. Radiant and glowing skin shows good health, vitality and personal care. Dull and tired looking skin shows an unhealthy lifestyle, stress and a lack of overall care. Natural beauty and skin is available for us all – it doesn't have to be in a salon, over a make-up counter, with a plastic surgeon or in a day spa – but in simple, affordable, remedies and ideas that anyone can follow.

Skin – reflecting what's on the inside

We can apply the most expensive skin lotions and potions to our skin, but still not have the vibrant, healthy skin that we want. This is because the most important factor in how we look on the outside is what we process through our bodies on the inside. This naturally refers to the food and drink that we consume, but also to other environmental factors such as the chemicals that we breathe into our systems – car emissions, carbon monoxide, detergents, cleaning products, fragrances etc.

Some of these factors are beyond our control, but we can certainly prevent unnecessary damage and strive to improve our physiological wellbeing in order to obtain young, healthy, radiant looking skin – literally treating our bodies from the "inside-out".

Skin-friendly food

By far the best start is to take a good look at what we eat. Research shows that a nutritionally-rich diet slows down the physiological ageing processes in all our tissues, including the skin. A balanced diet for fabulous skin should include all the nutrients needed to promote good health; protein, carbohydrates, fats, essential fatty acids and all the essential vitamins and minerals. Fresh foods are of optimum importance for your skin, the fresher the better.

Eat liberal amounts of fresh fruit and vegetables, which contain a wide variety of antioxidants; particularly important for the prevention of premature skin ageing. Seeds, nuts and grains, accompanied by protective foods like vegetable oils, yogurt, honey and yeast are all skin-friendly foods. Chicken, fish, eggs, turkey and soy are all good sources of protein and B vitamins. Our modern diets are often lacking in essential B vitamins which are pivotal to healthy hair, nails and skin.

Omega 3 is fantastic for great looking skin and can be found in fish such as wild salmon, sardines, mackerel and sild. Good skin is also a reflection of a well functioning digestive system. Boost sluggish assimilation by eating plenty of fibre, such as whole grains; swap white bread and pasta for wholemeal, white rice for brown and eat high fibre snacks, prunes, beans and legumes, apples and plenty of green leafy vegetables.

A well as eating the right foods, reduce types of food that can deprive the skin of moisture, such as alcohol and caffeine. Avoid processed food whenever possible as they often contain empty-calories, are high in salt and sugar content and lack the valuable nutrients that our bodies crave. Excess sugar is considered to cause premature ageing, damaging protein molecules in the skin and leading to a loss of skin elasticity, causing wrinkles and sagging.

If we invest in a nutritionally balanced diet, we will not only look better but also feel healthy and invigorated. When we feel healthy, we feel good about ourselves and this translates to how we interact with people around us. Try it, see if your nearest and dearest notice the difference!

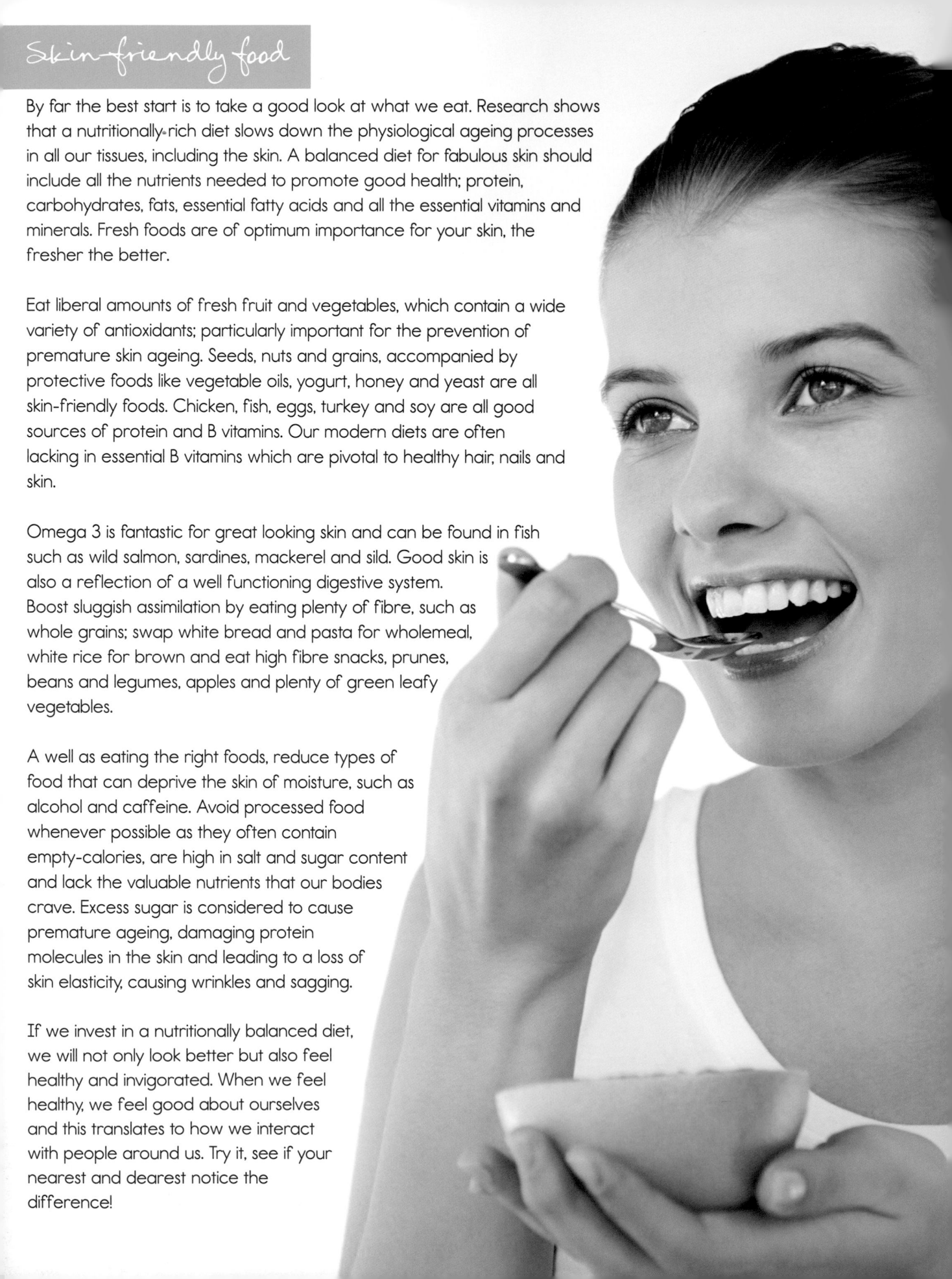

Blackheads

To loosen blackheads for easier removal, mix equal parts of baking soda and water in your hand and rub gently onto skin for 2 to 3 minutes. Rinse off with warm water.

Boost your circulation

Energise your skin, as well as your body and mind and get yourself moving! Sluggish circulation can affect how your skin looks, worsening bloating and puffiness, cellulite, acne, loss of muscle tone, and paleness. Exercise opens up blood vessels to make skin look healthy and youthful. Taking regular cardiovascular exercise increases blood flow to the skin which in turn assists the production of collagen.

So become more active, walk, jog, workout, go to the gym, take a class, even do stretches at work. As well as promoting good circulation physical exertion also helps us to de-stress, which is good for our overall health.

Cosmetics

Regularly replace your cosmetics and cosmetic brushes and sponges, including the sponge in your compact. Generally cosmestics don't have a shelf life of much longer than 6 months to a year, so no matter how tempted you are to hold on to that favourite mascara, renew your make-up regularly.

Drink lots of water

Water hydrates our bodies and purifies our insides, aiding the elimination process which will show through in how our skin looks. So remember your 8 glasses per day! Although, take care not drink too much fluid 2-3 hours before going to bed as this may contribute to morning puffiness.

Dry skin brushing

Dry skin brushing is another useful way to boost circulation and to stimulate the lymphatic system. Dry skin brushing exfoliates the skin, getting rid of dead skin cells and allowing the skin to detox more effectively. It also tightens skin, promotes removal of cellulite and increases skin renewal and rejuvenation. Best carried out just before taking a shower in the morning, you'll need a natural bristle brush, (not synthetic) preferably with a long handle in order to reach all parts of the body. Don't wet the skin beforehand as this stretches the skin. Start at the soles of the feet and work up your legs, to your abdomen, buttocks, back and lastly hands to arms. Brush the skin from each part of your body towards the heart.

When brushing the abdomen make circular anti-clockwise strokes, be gentle around the breast area and avoid the nipples. Brush each body part several times before showering or bathing in warm water. Rinse at the end with a cool rinse to invigorate circulation.

Dryness

Scratch a small area of skin on your arm with a fingernail, if it leaves a white mark then your skin is dry and needs exfoliating and moisturising.

Hands and feet

For luxuriously soft skin, use an intensive moisturising cream on your hands and feet at night and then wear thin-fabric gloves and socks. Keep them on overnight to achieve best results.

Ingredients

Skin products with ingredients containing fragrances, dyes and preservatives can be too harsh for certain skin types. Sensitive skin is particularly easily damaged and takes longer to recover. Be wary of alcohol-based products, as they can disturb the pH level of our complexions, leaving it dry and dehydrated.

Lose the flannel

Traditional washcloths and flannels are too abrasive to use on the face, so use your hands and fingers instead.

Mixing different skincare products

It's easy to collect an array of different skincare products, but probably not the most effective way to care for your skin.

You may be using products that contain the same ingredients, so are either on overkill or paying for something that you already have. It's better to stick with a good brand name and use their range of products.

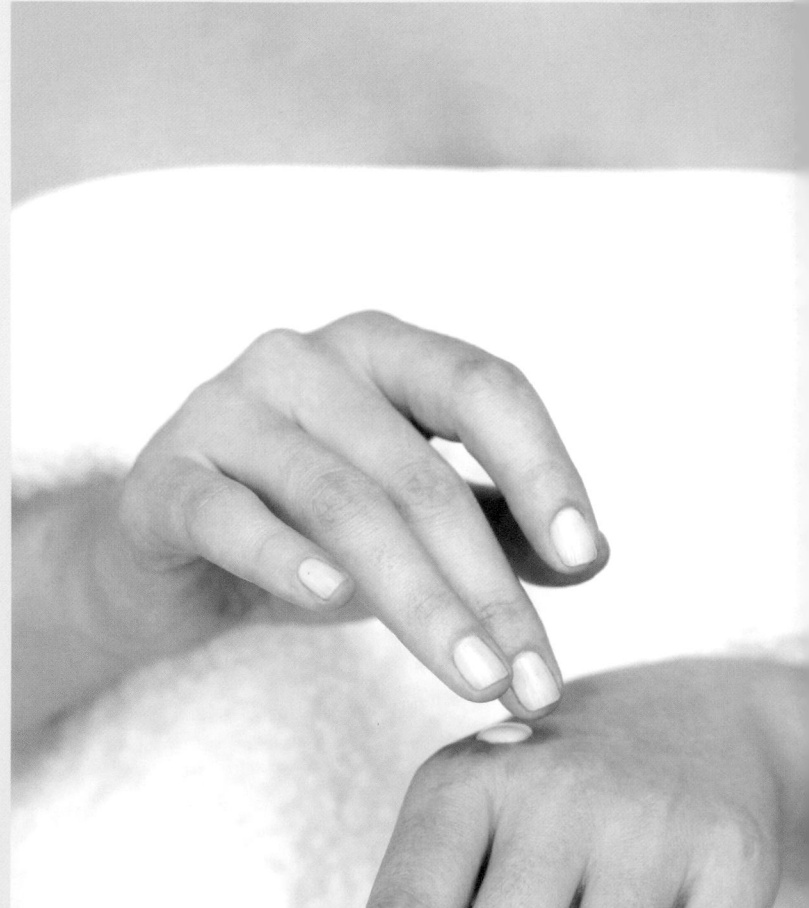

Moist, hot skin

To keep areas of the body that are prone to getting hot and sweaty, clean and dry, use un-perfumed baby powder. Areas such as underarms, inner thighs, bottom cheeks, under the breast area. This will prevent the growth of bacteria or fungi which can cause unpleasant skin conditions.

Natural born skin-killers!

To be avoided at all costs! Smoking, tanning salons, and sunbathing. Each of these horrors age the skin prematurely and lead to deep set facial lines - especially draw lines around the mouth area for smokers.

Olive oil

Massage a few drops over your face, backs of your arms, knees and elbows in the evening. This will moisten your skin beautifully.

Out in the sun

If you're out for a day in the sun, don't wear scented lotions and perfumes. This can lead to blotchy and itchy skin. Neither attractive, or comfortable!

Seasonal changes

During the winter our skin needs more moisture than summer, so reflect this in the products you use, i.e. a lighter moisturiser in summer and a heavier one for winter.

Sleep

Essential to our overall health, it is also vital to our skin because the majority of cell repair and regeneration occurs whilst we are sleeping. So if we're not getting enough kip our skin can't work effectively at repairing itself.

Steaming

Steam opens the skin's pores while deeply cleansing and rejuvenating all the skin's layers. Using herbs in facial steams is a great way to nourish your skin. Therapeutic herbs can be added to the water so that their healing benefits will become part of the steam and reach deep into your pores. Many herbs are emollient, softening and lubricating; others hydrate and moisturize; and most are antibacterial and anti-inflammatory.

Liquorice root is the number one herbal choice for steaming as it suits all skin types, by opening the pores, soothing, cleansing, and lubricating. As for other herbs, for dry skin try lavender or mint; for sensitve skin try chamomile and for oily skin try mint, lavender, rose and/or witch hazel.

Stop touching!

Our hands are usually our primary form of bodily contact, consequently they are a breeding ground for dirt and germs. When we touch our faces we're transferring the contents of our hands to our face! Not a pleasant thought, or at all good for our complexions.

Turn down the heat

Hot showers and baths strip skin of its moisture and wash away protective oils, so avoid using hot water and use lukewarm instead, to prevent over-drying of the skin.

Vitamins

Products containing vitamins are becoming increasingly more popular. Vitamin A, for fine lines and wrinkles, vitamin B for glowing skin and moisture retention, vitamin C for repairing sun damage and enhancing collagen production, vitamin E for powerful moisturising properties and repairing dry, rough skin and vitamin K for reducing dark circles under the eyes.

Wash your face

It is important to wash your face in the morning and at night. When we sleep yucky stuff like dead skin cells, dirt, and dust accumulates, so wash off the overnight nasties first thing in the morning!

Completely natural skin remedies

Apple Tonic (for all skin types)
Take a quarter cup of organic apple juice and apply to the face with a cotton ball. Leave for a few minutes then rinse. Apples contain a natural fruit acid which has an exfoliating effect. For oily skin add half a teaspoon of lime to the apple juice.

Avocado Moisturiser (for dry skin)
Take the skin of an avocado and smooth it all over your face, avoiding the eyes and nose. Allow to set for 15 minutes before rinsing off.

Banana and honey cream (for all skin types)
Mash 1/2 a banana, mix in 1 tablespoon honey and 2 tablespoons of sour cream. Apply to the face and allow to set for about 10 minutes, then gently rinse off.

Brown Sugar Body Exfoliant
Mix half a cup of brown sugar, 1 tablespoon of vitamin E oil and half a freshly squeezed orange in a bowl.

Stand in the bath or shower and wet your body. Taking handfuls of the mixture gently scrub over your body in circular motions. When all areas of the body have been scrubbed, rinse off and dry as normal. Apply a moisturising lotion once dried to prevent your skin dehydrating.

Cucumber & Kiwi Refresher (for all skin types)
Grate or blend half a cucumber and a kiwi and apply over the face and around the eyes. Leave for 15 to 20 minutes and rinse off.

Lime Juice Eye-Reviver
Take 4 tablespoons of lime juice and iced water. Saturate cotton pads in the mixture and place over closed eyelids for 10 minutes.

Milk & Honey Oatmeal Cleanser (for all skin types)
Mix 1/2 cup ground oatmeal, 1/2 cup milk and 1 tablespoon of honey. Once mixed, massage into the skin gently, then rinse off with lukewarm water. Refrigerate any remaining mixture after use.

Orange and Yogurt Vibrancy Mask (for combination skin)
Mix the grated rind of one orange with 1/2 cup of organic yogurt. Apply to the face and wait 10 minutes before rinsing off.

Strawberry Purifier (for oily skin)
Mix 1/4 cup pure aloe vera, 2 tablespoons of plain organic yoghurt, three crushed strawberries and 1/4 cup Borax. Once mixed, massage gently into skin then rinse off with lukewarm water

Summer skin care

Summer is one of the seasonal battles for maintaining good skin care! Summer may not have the harsh cold or winds of the winter, but it does have the punishing heat of the sun at it's maximum strength during the summer months. To reduce or avoid the effects of the sun's harmful rays, here are a few tips.

Using sunscreen product which has an SPF of 15 or above is essential for us all. Allowing yourself to bake in the midday sun, damages and prematurely ages skin – as well as increasing the risk of skin cancer. Use a complete sun-block of factor 50 for children. Research indicates that one or more severe sunburns in childhood significantly increase the risk of developing skin cancer later in life. Check the expiry date on your sunscreen. Sunscreen without an expiry date should not be kept for any longer than 3 years. Always wear a hat in the sun, preferably with a wide brim which will protect your face.

Always wear sunglasses which block 100% of the sun's UV rays. Most retail outlets sell sunglasses with a sticker showing the percentage of UV protection. These will protect your eyes and also the skin around them which is particularly thin. If you are wearing lightweight or lightly coloured fabrics use sunscreen under your clothing. Research has proven that the sun can penetrate lightweight and lighter coloured fabrics. And if you're not worried about being too hot, wear darker, tightly woven fabrics as these are much more effective at blocking UV rays.

Drink plenty of water, hot weather increases the risk of dehydration which can be very dangerous if an extreme case. If you are undertaking any form of exercise or other physical activity, have a drink before you start and keep drinking throughout. In addition to the health risks of dehydration your skin will take a hammering if your body is lacking essential water.

The incidence of skin cancer is on the increase and it is believed that many deaths that occur can be prevented via early detection. By taking the time to examine your skin monthly, you will become familiar with what is normal for you and where any blemishes and moles are located. It is useful to note down the dates of self-exams.

Check the entirety of your body, including the feet, between the toes and the whole of your head; including your ears and scalp. Use a mirror for parts of your body that are hard to see and make sure that the room has good visibility or is well-lit. Whilst you are looking at each area, use your hands to feel over your skin. If you are concerned about anything that you find, regardless of how small and how 'silly' you might feel, be sure to make an appointment with your Doctor and get yourself checked out.

Winter skin care

The cold climate brings with it a range of skin-nightmares - dry, rough, sore, flaky and itchy – not to mention chapped lips! Winter really is your skin's arch-enemy. Follow these tips to reduce the effects of winter on your skin.

Outside the temperature falls and inside the heating goes up! Central heating wreaks havoc on skin, eyes and nasal passages, drying them out and causing discomfort. Have the thermostat set to the lowest level that you can comfortably stand. If you have access to room humidifiers, these will help to balance out the moisture levels in the room. Drink lots of water. Internal hydration keeps skin cells plump and healthy.

Although most of us relish the thought of a hot bath or shower when it's cold, this will dry skin out more. Keep showers and baths short and use warm water, not hot. Use gentle skin products for your skin care, anything too harsh will worsen any already dry and sensitive skin.

Moisturising effectively is essential in winter, so a suitable moisturiser for your skin type is a must. Your winter moisturiser should be heavier than the one that you use for summer as your skin will crave more moisture in the cold. Pay attention to dry areas, hands, feet, elbows and knees so that they don't become cracked and painful.

You will still need protection from the sun in winter, even though it has lost its heat. Remember to protect your ears and lips also.

Exfoliate on a weekly basis with a gentle exfoliating product. This will remove dead skin cells and prevent your skin from looking grey and dull.

Haircare

Have you ever wondered how some people seem to achieve shiny, healthy, luscious looking hair, sporting an immaculate style which never looks out of place? Ever wondered why you can't achieve the same look? Well, healthy hair is not hard to achieve, or a best-kept secret that no-one has let you in on – all you need to do is learn a few natural, creative and clever hair care tips and you'll be the envy of your friends.

Natural haircare solutions

Avocado

Known for its beneficial proteins and hydrating properties, mash one avocado and mix it with 1 tablespoon of lemon juice, 1 teaspoon of sea salt and 1 tablespoon of pure aloe vera. Mix the ingredients until they turn into a paste and then comb through your hair with your fingers. Cover with a plastic shower cap, (or bag), and wrap a towel around your head. Leave for 20-30 minutes before rinsing out the paste and shampooing as normal.

Baking soda

Need to remove grease, dirt and the gunk of products from your hair without adding even more gunk to it? Add 1 tablespoon of baking soda to your hair while shampooing and it will remove all those nasty chemicals that styling products deposit.

Beer

For a boost of life for your hair use some flat beer. Mix 3 tablespoons of beer in a half cup of warm water and after shampooing and rinsing your hair, rub in the mix gently and leave for a couple of minutes before rinsing it off.

Butter

As a remedy to dry, damaged hair use butter for a glorious shine! Take a small knob of butter and massage it into your dry hair. Cover your hair over with a shower cap for half an hour and then shampoo and rinse as normal.

Castor Oil

For maximum shine for dull hair, mix up 2 teaspoons of castor oil, 1 teaspoon glycerine and one egg white. Massage the mixture into wet hair and wash out after a few minutes.

Espresso

For extra shine make one cup of strong espresso and let it cool. Pour the liquid over your dry hair and leave for 20 minutes. Rinse out as normal.

Lemon juice

Lemon juice mixed with water can be used as a last rinse to give your hair added shine and bounce.

Mayonnaise

For an effective way to condition your hair and give it a naturally gorgeous shine, use a dollop of mayonnaise and massage it into your hair and scalp. Cover your head with a shower cap and wait a few minutes before shampooing out.

Olive Oil

A sleek and fashionable method of putting back much needed moisture and lustre into dry, brittle hair. Apply half a cup of warm, (not hot!), olive oil to your hair, making sure that you massage it well into your hair and scalp. Cover your hair with a cap and leave for 45 minutes before shampooing and rinsing as normal.

Tea

For an old fashioned hair remedy said to add a natural shine to hair, use a litre of warm tea, (without the sugar or milk!), as your final rinse after shampooing.

Vinegar

To make a great conditioner that will inject life into limp or lifeless hair, mix 1 teaspoon of apple cider vinegar, 3 egg whites and 2 tablespoons of olive oil. Massage the mixture into your hair, cover with a cap and leave for 30 minutes before shampooing and rinsing.

Afro hair or extra curly hair
Avoid using brushes on these types of hair as this can cause damage by pulling out hair from the scalp or breaking the hair part way down. Instead, use a wide toothed comb or even your fingers to work through your hair.

Drink water
Drinking plenty of water will hydrate your skin, body and hair. Dehydration will show on your scalp and in the condition of your hair, so do your best to drink the recommend 8 glasses per day.

Healthy diet
The well-coined phrase "You are what you eat" extends to the condition and health of your hair. For shiny, glowing hair a well balanced diet with plenty of proteins and vitamins will keep your hair and scalp in optimum condition, from the inside out. Vitamins such as biotin, vitamin E, vitamin B and vitamin C are believed to boost hair growth and condition.

Heat protection
Our hair beauty regimes consist of hairdryers, straighteners, curlers, heated rollers and all manner of heat-based methods of styling. Naturally, this dries hair out, stripping it of moisture and leaving hair frazzled, hard to style and worst of all, breaking off. Before using a hairdryer, pat your hair dry with a towel and let the remaining moisture in your hair dry naturally, leaving your hair damp and reducing the amount of blow-drying time. To further minimise the damage caused by heat styling use a good heat protection product. These can be sourced in good hair salons and it might be useful to ask for advice in purchasing the right product for your hair.

Massage
Massaging your scalp increases the blood flow, nourishing the roots and stimulating hair growth. Some hair and beauty salons offer head massages as part of their treatments. An excellent opportunity to relax, as well as good for your scalp and hair!

Moisturise
For essential moisturising treatment use either a conditioner especially for intense conditioning at least once a week, or alternatively one of the moisturising natural remedies detailed in this section. Apply to your hair as normal, but leave on and cover with a shower cap for between 10-20 minutes, (or the recommended treatment time). This will ensure that your hair absorbs valuable moisture, leaving your hair well conditioned and soft to touch.

Product build-up
Too much product in your hair will make it look heavy, tired and dirty. Use a natural method of cleansing product build-up for a fresh start and don't overdo it with products going forward. Generally one product to style and one to give it a last minute finish should be plenty. Avoid applying hair styling products directly onto your scalp, as this will clog the pores on your head.

Products to suit

Greasy, dry, frizzy, combination, coloured, permed, heat damaged, blonde, brunette, redhead… there are so many products to choose from. Where do you start? General rule of thumb is that if your hair is easy to manage, looks shiny, feels healthy and most importantly, you are happy with it – then you must be doing something right and it's likely that the products that you are using suit your hair type. If this isn't the case then it's possible that you need to change your hair products. Avoid using hair styling products containing alcohol, which dries out hair.

Natural ingredients

If you prefer your hair-care to include natural ingredients look out for products which contain essential oils, vegetable oils and herbs. Essential oils such as lavender and tea tree have naturally antiseptic properties in them and help in the treatment of dandruff. Rosemary and ylang-ylang are believed to aid hair growth. Vegetable oils such as safflower, soya bean and olive oil are fantastic for moisturising and conditioning hair.

Professional cuts

For an instantly healthier look for your hair a good professional haircut is a must-have. Split-ends will be removed, your style will be revitalised; or even changed completely! Getting help and advice on the right texture, colour, style and hair length for you is important, and as your crowning glory you owe it to yourself to give your hair the best treatment possible. Regular trims with your stylist will make your hair look as fabulous as you'll feel.

Sleep

Use a satin pillowcase to cut down on hair rubbing and fly-away hair! Avoid sleeping in hair accessories such as scrunchies, etc. as these can lead to hair damage. Elastic bands are an absolute NO at any time of day!.

Problem solved!

Split ends

Split ends, or 'Trichoptlosis' as it is professionally known– the bane of many a woman's life! This is a widespread condition affecting the ends of hair fibres where the protective cuticle has been stripped away, causing ends to split into 2 to 3 parts. The most effective treatment is to cut off the split end fibre. Typically most people think this is an issue primarily for long hair, but people with short hair can be just as prone if their hair is in bad condition. Causes include not trimming the hair often enough, over-exposure to the sun and heat-damage generated by heat styling products, colouring and waving causing drying out of the hair shaft, chlorine in swimming baths, overly vigorous brushing or back-combing, poor quality brushes/combs and a lack of natural oils reaching the end of the hair shaft; particularly in long hair. The worst thing we can do with split ends is to ignore them. Every time you brush your hair the ends will split more, eventually breaking off and making your hair shorter and shorter, and in dreadful condition.

Useful tips for split ends

First and foremost – ensure that you book in for a trim regularly. A nightmare for anyone growing their hair, but even the tiniest trim will help your hair look healthier and thicker whilst it's growing. And it will avoid the angst of having to lose a few inches of badly split hair once you're 6-months down the line! Ask your stylist to recommend specialist products which can temporarily seal the splits and catch any potential splits before they occur. Regimentally deep condition your hair at least once a week. Avoid using heat styling where possible and don't over brush or comb your hair. Invest in quality brushes and combs. Be gentle with your hair! Shampoo and condition your hair after a workout or strenuous exercise. The salt contained in perspiration erodes the hair shaft, causing brittle hair and split ends. Buy a good protective conditioner, which is specially designed for swimming in chlorine.

Dandruff

Dandruff is quite simply the shedding of dead skin from your scalp at a faster rate than normal, causing white flakes and itching of the scalp. Everyone experiences having a degree of dandruff at one time or another.

The causes of dandruff vary and can include hormone imbalance, poor nutrition or health, improper rinsing-out of shampoo, lack of sleep, stress, exhaustion, poor hygiene, overuse of styling products, excessive cold or heat, allergic reactions.

Although there is no 'cure' for dandruff, there are ways in which you can control and limit its re-occurrence.

Useful tips for eliminating dandruff

The most important consideration in the treatment of this dandruff is to keep the hair and scalp clean so as to reduce the accumulation of dead cells on the scalp.

For mild dandruff, shampooing your hair with a mild shampoo daily should help. Be sure to wash your hair thoroughly, but gently, and ensure all of the shampoo is washed out. Don't use strong shampoos as this can dry out your hair and irritate your scalp, making the dandruff worse.

If this doesn't help, try anti-dandruff shampoo. Lather and rinse your hair twice, the first wash will clean your scalp, the second will medicate it. You should see an improvement within a couple of weeks. Your local pharmacy should be able to advise you on which products to use. For a more natural approach, a teaspoon of fresh lime juice used in the last rinse is believed to be an effective remedy, not only leaving the hair shiny and glowing, but removing any sticky products and preventing dandruff.

Choosing the right hairstyle for your face

There are literally thousands of ways in which we can style our hair, but due to our own unique set of facial features and shapes we know that not all of us can wear long flowing tresses, or that short elf-like-hair-do that looks so feminine on the girl on the magazine cover, but makes us look positively boyish in reality! So, how can we make the most of our features and our face shapes? None of our faces are equal – thin, rounded, angular, soft, long, square. We need to accentuate the positive and draw away from facial features we don't like.

Angular Features

To draw away from a sharp or angular face shape, or features, create a curly or wavy hairstyle to soften.

Heart shape face

Face is wide at the temples and hairline, narrowing to a small delicate chin.
Try chin-length or longer hairstyles and side partings. Layers that are swept forward around the upper part of the face, with a wispy fringe will achieve a more balanced look by giving your face fullness where it needs it.

High forehead

A full fringe lying horizontally across the forehead will cover the forehead area.

Low forehead

Soft fullness at the crown area and vertical lines can help to lengthen the face.

Large Nose

Wearing a full hairstyle, whether layered or curls, or an upswept crown make a larger nose less prominent.

Narrow chin

Wearing long hair with fullness or curls at the chin will make the chin seem wider.

Oval face

Slightly narrower at the jawline than at the temples, with a gently rounded hairline.
Luckily, this face shape can wear almost any hairstyle! The even proportion of an oval face gives a balanced look which suits long, short or medium length hairstyles. Just avoid heavy fringes and styles that are brushed onto the face.

Round face

Full-looking face with a round chin and hairline. Widest point is at the cheeks and ears.
Introducing a side parting in the hair will slim and lengthen the face. A hairstyle with fullness and height at the crown, whilst keeping the rest of your hair relatively close to your head, will make your face seem longer and narrower.

Square face or full chin

A strong, square jawline and usually an equally square hairline.
A short hairstyle with fullness or soft curls at the crown area will detract attention from the chin area. To soften the square appearance of the face, wear layers and wispy looks. If your hair is straight maybe invest in a body wave, as waves and curls will create an attractive balance to the straight features of your face shape.

Thin face

Long and slender, about the same width at forehead and just below cheekbones.
In need of widening, wearing curls or fullness at the sides will create a wider look. Avoid long hair, which will make the face look longer and thinner.

10 Minute Makeover

If you're constantly battling with time and have no space to commit to a lengthy beauty regime, this may be just what you need. These 10-minute beauty shortcuts are great for a busy lifestyle, optimising precious spare time whilst making you look and feel a million dollars.

10-Minute morning routine

Avoid morning mayhem with these easy to follow tips for looking your best.

Cleanse and moisturise

There are a myriad of products and recommended cleansing routines available. But if you're stretched for time, invest in a gentle cleansing bar or foaming cleanser, and indulge in an old-fashioned wash with warm water.

There are plenty of soaps and foaming cleansers formulated to be kinder to skin and respect your skin's natural acidity.

This is a quick, easy and less messy alternative to creams and lotions. They're also easy to rinse off and a final splash of cold water will bring colour to your cheeks, firm your skin and act as a refreshing 'wake-up'. Massage in your usual brand of moisturiser to hydrate and soften your skin.

Cheeks

A hint of colour on the cheeks gives your face a healthy glow first thing in the morning.

Smile in the mirror and apply your blush to the apple of your cheek, sweeping it back towards the cartilage nub in your ear. Applied too low blusher will make your face look wider.

Eyes

Our eyes are the first thing that people notice about us, and this is certainly true first thing in the morning when we're regaining wakefulness after a full night's sleep.

Once you've washed and moisturised, a light coating of mascara on the upper lashes will open the eye up and make you look more awake.

There are great lengthening products on the market if you want to achieve a longer, fuller lash look.

Lips

In the morning, using a slightly damp toothbrush, very lightly scrub your lips to remove any dry flakes. This will also stimulate the circulation giving you rosy, warm looking lips. Add a little lip salve to moisten your lips.

Hair

For mid to long hair, if you're pressed for time you can just pull it back into a ponytail or with clips. Use a non-stick hairspray to tame fly-away hair.

Scent

To finish off, use a body spray or a little perfume. Something light and fresh, you don't want to overpower anyone!

Skin

It's rare that we can get up, look at our skin and be completely happy with what we see in front of us. Most of us have something that we want to cover up or disguise, whether it be blemishes, spots, broken capillaries or dark circles. Rather than cover the whole of your face with foundation, just touch up any areas of concern with a foundation that best suits your skin tone. If you're in a particular rush, you could try mixing your moisturiser with your foundation – saving you having to put on two products. Either that or invest in a tinted moisturiser.

5-Minute make-up tips

Tips for times when you have only minutes to get a great look and get out the door:-

- Apply an all-in-one foundation and powder product; this will give your skin the right amount of coverage – and in half the time.

- Buy 2-in-1 products that can be applied on cheeks and lips, or cheeks and eyes. These keep your colour tones similar and save time.

- For a quick, effective eye opener, apply a shiny highlighter below the arch of the brow and in the inner corner of the eyelid. This will open and lift the eye.

- Cream eye shadow applied straight from stick is quick, easy and stays on.

- One coat of mascara is enough for top and bottom lashes. Invest in good quality, opthalmic approved mascara for optimum looks.

- Using a brow pencil, define your eyebrows to give your face more definition and impact.

- A touch of powder blush can be applied using a big blusher brush for a fast, effective look. Sweep up from your cheek towards your eyes.

- To create the illusion of a slimmer face use bronzers and highlighters. Sweep some bronzer under your cheekbones and apply a highlighter above your cheekbones, then blend together.

- For a healthy glowing look dust some bronzer onto your brow bone, nose and chin.

- Use a neutral colour or translucent lipstick for a faster application and a natural look. Less precision is needed and no lip-liner.

- Shaking off any excess, dab a translucent powder with a velour puff over your face to prevent shine and finish off your make-up.

- Use disposable make-up remover wipes for removing eye shadow and mascara. Baby wipes are just as good!

5-Minute essential basics

Tips essential to our everyday beauty routine:-

Cleanser
Dermatologists recommend that a gentle cleanser is the most effective way to cleanse your face. So if you're a die-hard scrubbing with soap and water person then you may want to revise your thinking. Over-washing or vigorous washing can strip away the skin's natural barriers and moisture. Washing with a gentle cleansing product no more than twice a day is the kindest way to cleanse your skin.

Have the right beauty tools
There's not much point in spending a small fortune on the best beauty products but not investing in the right tools to apply them with! Any large department store will stock full ranges of beauty tools and brushes sets.

Lips
How many of us take our lip-care for granted? They're one of the most sensual features on our faces, and one that comes into regular contact with other people! Considering their high-profile function we don't spend nearly enough time looking after our lips and enhancing their natural beauty. The number one rule for lips is to keep them hydrated and moist. Prevent dry and cracked lips with lip balm, use a balm with an added SPF when outside. Use lip balm during the day and before you go to bed at night. For a gentle, natural looking pout apply a little petroleum jelly to your lips and rub it in. Follow with lip balm.

Moisturise
If you have time for nothing else in your daily routine, prioritise time to moisturise. The type and brand of moisturiser will depend upon your skin type, individual needs and preferences, but never underestimate the importance of moisturising. Moisturisers plump up and smooth the skin and protect us, to some degree, from premature ageing. Start using moisturisers young and reap the benefits in later years.

Sunscreen
Most of us know that sunscreens help reduce the risk of skin cancer, but they are also a vital beauty ingredient in keeping our skin looking young. The sun adversely affects the amount of collagen production in the skin, which is essential in maintaining plump, moist, youthful skin. Not only does sun damage cause more wrinkles and fine lines, but also more freckles, age spots, and spider veins. Skin can also start to look rough and leathery, or loose and saggy because of sun exposure. Sunscreen with an SPF of 15 or over can protect skin from the sun's damaging rays, so that even if you spend time outdoors your face is less likely to suffer sun damage and add unnecessary years to your age.

5-Minute facial workouts

A non-invasive way to help to firm up skin, maintain good circulation and achieve a radiant, youthful look to your face and complexion:-

Double-chin buster
Sit at a table and, with a closed, relaxed mouth jut your chin forward and slightly upwards. Rest one elbow on the table and clench your fist. Balance your chin on your clenched fist. Slide your lower lip out and over your top lip. Press the tip of your tongue against the roof of your mouth behind your top teeth. Increase the pressure over a count of 5 hold the position. Slowly release the pressure. Repeat the sequence 3 times.

Forehead firmer
Raise your muscles above your eyebrows and gently but firmly use your fingers to smooth out the forehead wrinkles. Repeat the sequence 3 times before raising and dropping your eyebrows quickly 20 times.

Lip conditioner
Imagine you're playing to a room full of adoring fans and blow 10 kisses in quick succession. Then repeat by pressing two fingers lightly against your lips and blowing 10 more kisses. A really fun way to firm lips!

Firm droopy eyelids
Look straight ahead and place your index finger lengthwise just under your eyebrows. Keeping your eyes open, gently push up your eyebrows and hold them firmly against the bone. Slowly close your eyes and feel the pull between brow and lashes. Squeeze your eyes tightly together and hold for 5 seconds. Release the pressure over another count of 5. Repeat the sequence 3 times. Soothe tired eyes with a cooling eye mask.

Jaw and neckline workout
Jut your chin upward so that you can feel that the front of your neck is taut. Push your lower lip over your top lip towards your nose. Keeping your neck stretched, slowly smile by pulling the corners of your mouth upward and outward over a count of 5 seconds. Hold this position for another count of 5 and firmly stroke the jaw-line upwards with the flats of your hands. Release the position slowly over a count of 5. Repeat the sequence 3 times.

Super fast tips to achieve super looks:-

Test new foundations on your cheek not on your hands. Our hands are darker on the back and paler on the inside.

Don't have time for a tan? Invest in some bronzing powder for your face and shoulders.

Use neutral shades and you won't have to worry about your cosmetics clashing with your clothing.

Lip colours – the deeper or brighter the colour the more obvious it will be when it starts to fade. If you don't have time to re-apply endlessly stick to a safer, more subtle tone.

Periodically sharpen all of your make-up pencils so you're not fishing for the sharpener at the last minute.

For blobbed and clogged mascara use a clean, damp mascara wand to separate out the clogged lashes, and a damp cotton bud to clean blobs up from the surrounding area.

Add a finishing touch to your lips with lip-gloss, giving you the appearance of plumper, more luscious looking lips. Keep it in your purse for touch ups!

Foundation sunk into your skin creases? Use a cotton bud to clean out and re-blend.

Overdone the eye shadow? Blend a tiny dot of concealer on the centre of your lids to calm the colour.

The skin on your chest will show signs of ageing just as much as your face and neck, don't neglect this zone and moisturise daily.

Bronzing powders make good blusher substitutes if needed. Choose the bronzer according to your complexion.

Strengthen weak and brittle nails by using a good nail hardener. Massage oil into the nail base daily and moisturise well.

Rub a slick of vaseline along your eyebrows, in the direction of hair growth, to keep in good shape and condition hairs.

The ideas and recipes contained in this book are passed on in good faith but the publisher cannot be held responsible for any adverse results. It is also recommended that you consult your doctor before embarking on any fitness regime or eating programme.

This edition first published in 2009 by ImPulse Paperbacks, an imprint of Iron Press Ltd. © Iron Press Ltd 2009 Printed in China